P9-CEH-917

Welcome!

All of the ingredients in this book are safe to use, but make sure you always follow these rules...

Before You Start

- Read the instructions before starting, and follow them carefully.
- Gather all the ingredients and equipment before you start.
- Don't use any ingredients not listed in the recipes and make sure an adult has checked them over before you start sliming.
- Any slime making should be done under adult supervision. We've highlighted times when a grown up should do something for you.
- No snacking around the slime-making area and when we say slimes cannot be eaten – we mean it! Only ever eat the edible slimes. If you're not sure if you can eat it - check the warning box. We recommend you eat it within 24 hours – it won't taste as yummy otherwise!
- Keep children under 3 years old and all animals away from your slime experiments.
- Wear eye protection and keep slimy hands away from your eyes.
- Only make and play with slime on hard surfaces – keep away from furniture, carpets, and other delicate items that are hard to clean.
- Always store your slime in an airtight container (see p64) and place in the fridge. Throw it away after a week.
- Watch out when using paint or food colouring – it can stain. Wear rubber gloves so you don't stain your hands.
- Always wash your hands before and after making and playing with slime.
- Clean up after yourself! Wash all equipment and surfaces (see p64).
- A lot of the slimes use eyewash solution. Make sure you use this and not lens cleaner or contact lens solution.
- Don't handle poster paint for too long and wash your hands immediately after using them.

the SLIME book

Editors Elizabeth Yeates and Clare Lloyd
US senior editor Shannon Beatty
US editor Christy Lusiak
Jacket design Elle Ward
Pre-production producer
Dragana Puvacic
Senior producer Isabell Schart
Creative director Helen Senior
Cover photography Simon Pask
Photography Tim Pestridge
Publisher Sarah Larter

Written, designed, edited, and project-managed for DK by Dynamo Ltd.

First American Edition, 2017
Published in the United States by DK Publishing
345 Hudson Street, New York, New York 10014

17 18 19 20 21 10 9 8 7 6 5 4 3 2 1
001–309885–Dec/2017

Published in Great Britain by Dorling Kindersley Limited

A catalog record for this book is available from the Library of Congress.
ISBN: 978-1-4654-7373-8

DK books are available at special discounts when purchased in bulk for sales promotions, premiums, fund-raising, or educational use. For details, contact: DK Publishing Special Markets, 345 Hudson Street, New York, New York 10014
SpecialSales@dk.com

Printed and bound in China

A WORLD OF IDEAS:
SEE ALL THERE IS TO KNOW

www.dk.com

Acknowledgments:

The publisher would like to thank the following people for their help in photographing, designing, making, and handling slime: Tim Pestridge, Elissa Rowson, Olivia Chin-Yue, Mia Pestridge, Leo Sandford, and Bridget Stanley. Special thanks to Evie Allan for inspiring us to create this book.

Contents

Nonedible Slime

Edible Slime

Basic Slime Kit

These are the essentials needed for most of the recipes in this book...

Here are some of the extras you'll need. Check each recipe for specific ingredients.

Most ingredients in this book are easy to find, but if you can't get certain items, ask an adult to buy them or order them online.

Nonedible Slime

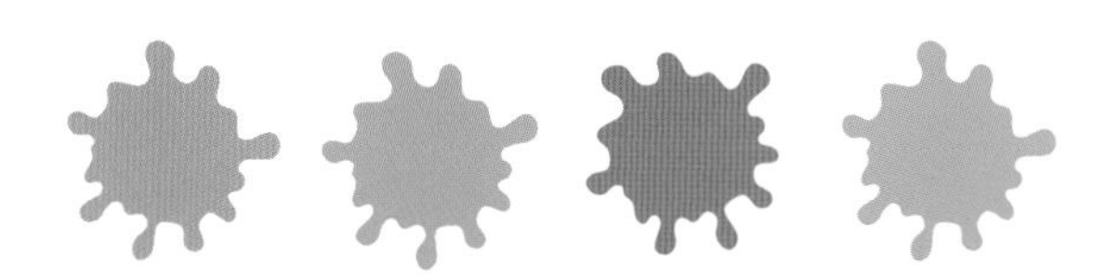

Yuk! Don't be tempted to eat these. We love making a slime mess, but make sure you clear up anything you may spill or drop. Ready? The slime fun is just over the page...

Basic Slime

TIME:
5 MINUTES

DIFFICULTY:
EASY

WARNING:
NONEDIBLE

This is the easiest recipe, but one of the most amazing. Watch as your slime turns from a solid to a liquid and back again in seconds!

YOU WILL NEED

- **cornstarch**
- **water**
- **food coloring**

1

Scoop a few big spoonfuls of cornstarch into a bowl.

2

Add drops of water little by little until you have a thick slime.

3

Grab a handful of slime and squish together. Keep your hands moving to keep the mixture solid. When you stop, the slime will change back into a liquid.

Stir in a few drops of food coloring for a blast of color.
MAY STAIN!

SCIENCE BIT

If you try to hit this slime, it will act like a solid and you'll get sore knuckles. If you gently poke your finger inside the mixture, it will feel like a liquid. Strange, huh? Hundreds of years ago famous scientist Sir Isaac Newton wrote about how liquids behave. Slime like this is known as a non-Newtonian fluid because it doesn't play by his rules!

Stretchy Slime

TIME:
10 MINUTES

DIFFICULTY:
EASY

WARNING:
NONEDIBLE

This is a super fun recipe to try. This gloopy stuff is the basis for many more awesome slimes later in the book.

YOU WILL NEED

- *1 cup PVA glue*
- *1 tsp baking soda*
- *finger paint or food coloring of your choice*
- *1 tbsp saline solution—it must contain boric acid or sodium borate*

1

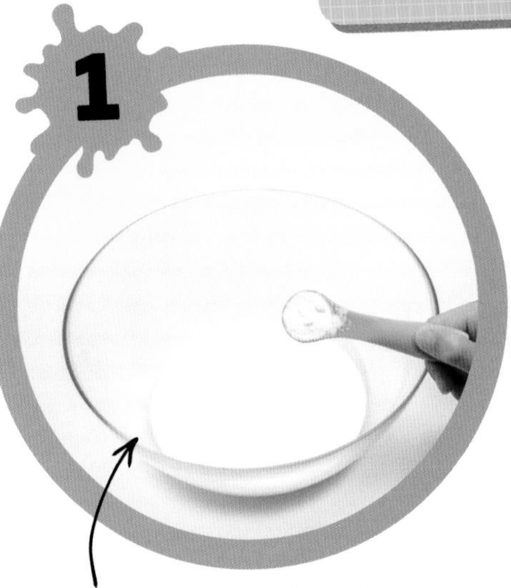

Pour the glue and baking soda into your bowl. Beat together.

2

Squirt in some paint and stir well. Keep adding more paint until you get the perfect color.

3

Drop in the saline solution and mix together. The slime will begin to get stringy. When it comes away from the edges of the bowl, knead or squish the mixture with your hands.

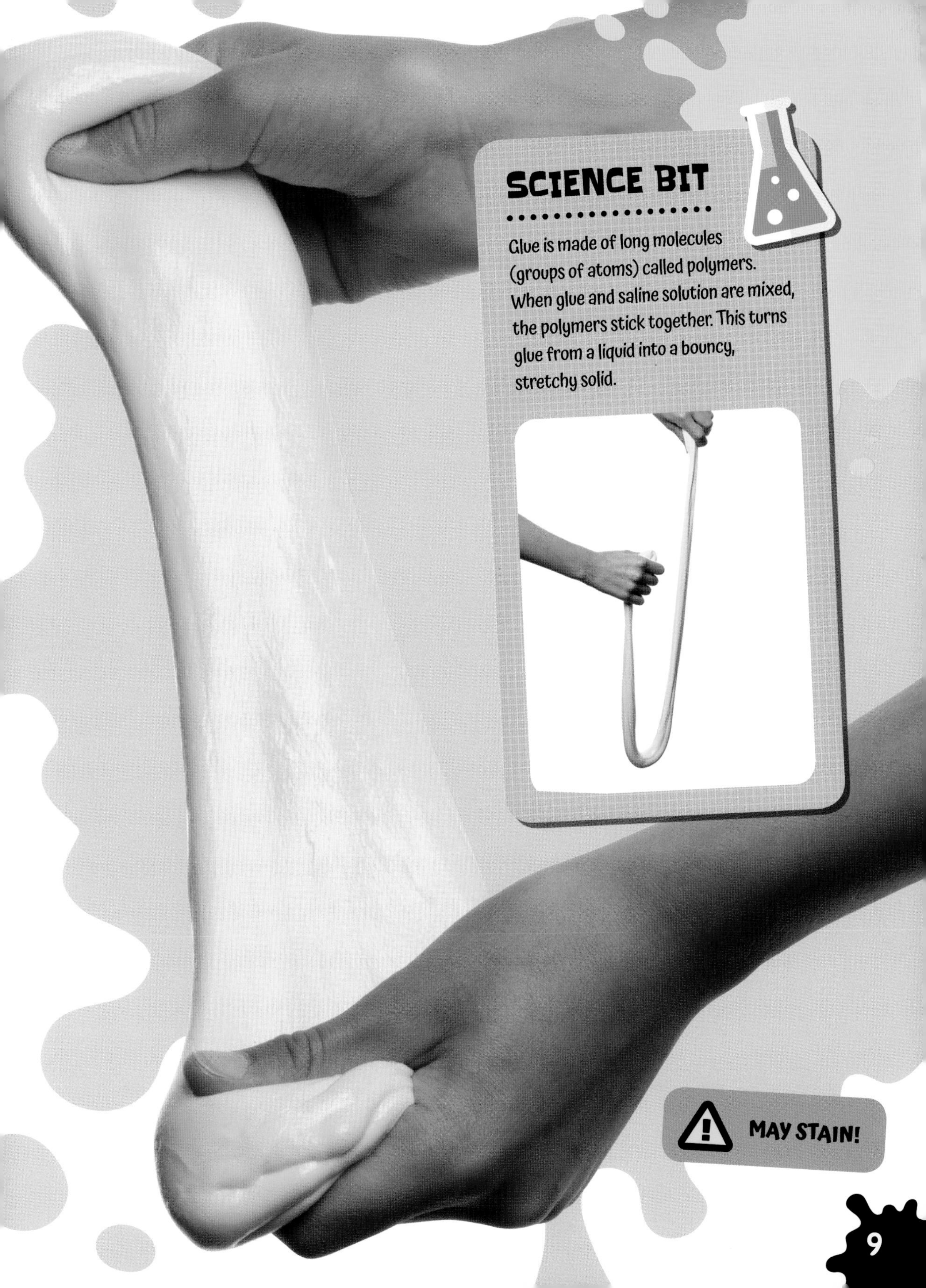

SCIENCE BIT

Glue is made of long molecules (groups of atoms) called polymers. When glue and saline solution are mixed, the polymers stick together. This turns glue from a liquid into a bouncy, stretchy solid.

MAY STAIN!

Fluffy Slime

TIME:
10 MINUTES

DIFFICULTY:
EASY

WARNING:
NONEDIBLE

Beat up a storm with this super-soft, foamy recipe. It might feel like clouds of marshmallow, but this slime is NOT to eat!

YOU WILL NEED

- 2 cups shaving cream (not gel)
- food coloring
- ¼ cup PVA glue
- ¼ tsp baking soda
- 1 tbsp saline solution—it must contain boric acid or sodium borate

1

Mix together the shaving cream and a few drops of food coloring. Then stir in the glue and the baking soda. Make sure it's all fully blended.

2

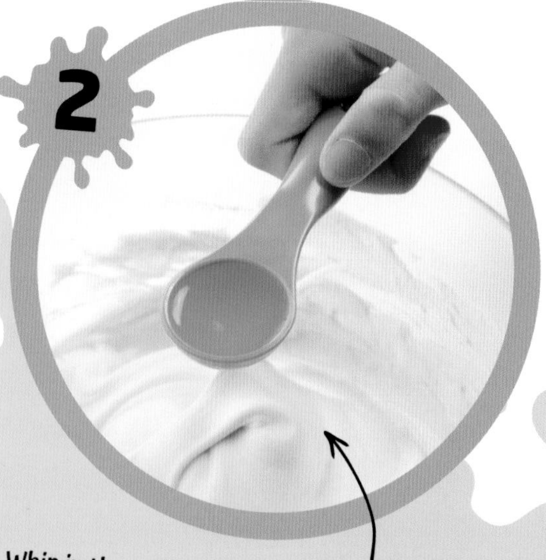

Whip in the saline solution. When the mixture starts to get stringy, you're almost there.

3

Now it's time to get your hands dirty! Knead the slime until it's puffy and soft. Add more saline solution if your mixture is too sticky.

SCIENCE BIT

Shaving cream is rather special. At different times it can be a gas, a liquid, or a solid. Inside the can, it's a gas. When squirted out, it's a solid. Over time, the foam turns into a liquid. Not many things can do that!

MAY STAIN!

See-through Slime

Good slime comes to those who wait. Hang on in there for a week as the bubbles slowly burst. Then it will be clear to see why this is also known as glass slime.

YOU WILL NEED

- ½ tsp baking soda
- ½ cup warm water
- ⅔ cup clear craft glue
- saline solution—it must contain boric acid or sodium borate

SCIENCE BIT

Some animals make slime, too. Hagfish create a thick, gloopy, see-through ooze to put attackers off. For this reason they are sometimes known as snot eels!

1

Put the baking soda and water into your bowl.

2

Mix in the clear glue. Then stir in small amounts of saline solution until the mixture starts to gloop together.

Keep mixing until your slime forms a big, see-through ball with bubbles inside. Check your slime every day until the bubbles have disappeared, and then play!

Serious Putty

TIME:
15 MINUTES

DIFFICULTY:
EASY

WARNING:
NONEDIBLE

Have fun making this simple two-ingredient recipe. Once you've made this super soft and stretchy slime, you won't be able to stop playing with it!

YOU WILL NEED

* reusable sticky tack
* liquid hand soap

1

Take a strip of sticky tack. Stretch the tack and play with it until it softens.

TOP TIP!

You can fold in some splashes of food coloring, but watch out—it can go everywhere! It will also stain your fingers, so make sure you wear rubber gloves.

Pour some liquid soap into a small bowl. Dip the tack into the liquid soap and squish it together.

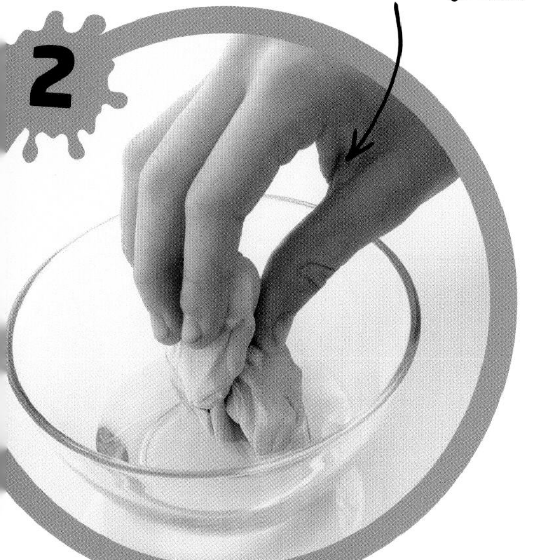

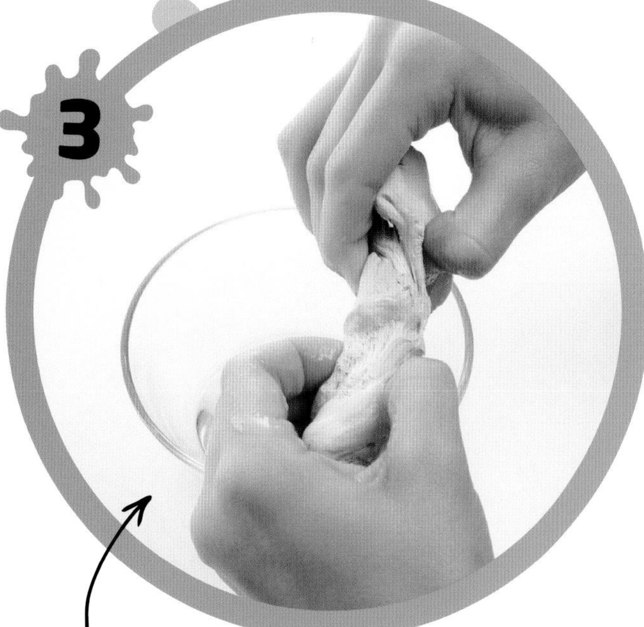

Continue to dip the tack into the liquid soap and work together. You will find the tack becomes more stretchy as you go. Don't add too much soap or the putty will become sticky.

Starry Slime

TIME:
10 MINUTES

DIFFICULTY:
EASY

WARNING:
NONEDIBLE

A sprinkle of neon sparkle will give this slime an out-of-this world shine.

YOU WILL NEED

- ½ tsp baking soda
- ½ cup warm water
- ⅔ cup clear craft glue
- neon purple glitter
- saline solution—it must contain boric acid or sodium borate
- star confetti
- star glitter

MAY STAIN!

How about...?

This is a great slime to make at a birthday party. Instead of star confetti, grab bags of number confetti—for how old you're going to be!

1

Mix together the baking soda, water, and clear glue. Pour neon glitter on top. You shouldn't need food coloring. The glitter should be enough to add color and sparkle.

2

Stir in small splashes of saline solution until the slime doesn't stick to your fingers.

3

Add star confetti and more glitter. To give your slime real depth, try to find stars of different sizes. Mix everything together with your hands, and play!

Crunchy Slime

TIME:
10 MINUTES

DIFFICULTY:
EASY

WARNING:
NONEDIBLE

Use this recipe to make some seriously gruesome goo with added crunch! Why not make this slime at Halloween?

YOU WILL NEED

- **½ tsp baking soda**
- **½ cup warm water**
- **⅔ cup clear craft glue**
- **red food coloring**
- **saline solution—it must contain boric acid or sodium borate**
- **plastic beads**

1

Mix baking soda, water, and clear glue. Add a few drops of red food coloring and stir.

2

Drop in a little saline solution at a time. Beat the mixture together until it stops sticking to the bowl.

3

Add a handful or two of plastic beads. Fold them into the slime using your hands. Let the gory fun begin!

TOP TIP!

The beads will make a crunching noise as they grind against each other. See how many you can put into your slime mix and find out how the sound changes.

MAY STAIN!

Smelly Slime

Slime looks good and feels good, so now it's time to find out how to make it smell good, too!

YOU WILL NEED

- 1 cup PVA glue
- 1 tsp baking soda
- red and yellow finger paint
- a few drops of your choice of food flavoring
- 1 tbsp saline solution—it must contain boric acid or sodium borate

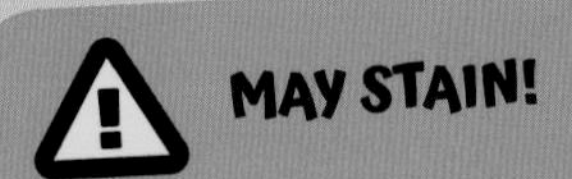

TOP TIP!

As yummy as this slime smells, don't be tempted to take a quick bite! Why not make a trick slime that doesn't smell so nice? Try combining food flavoring that shouldn't go together!

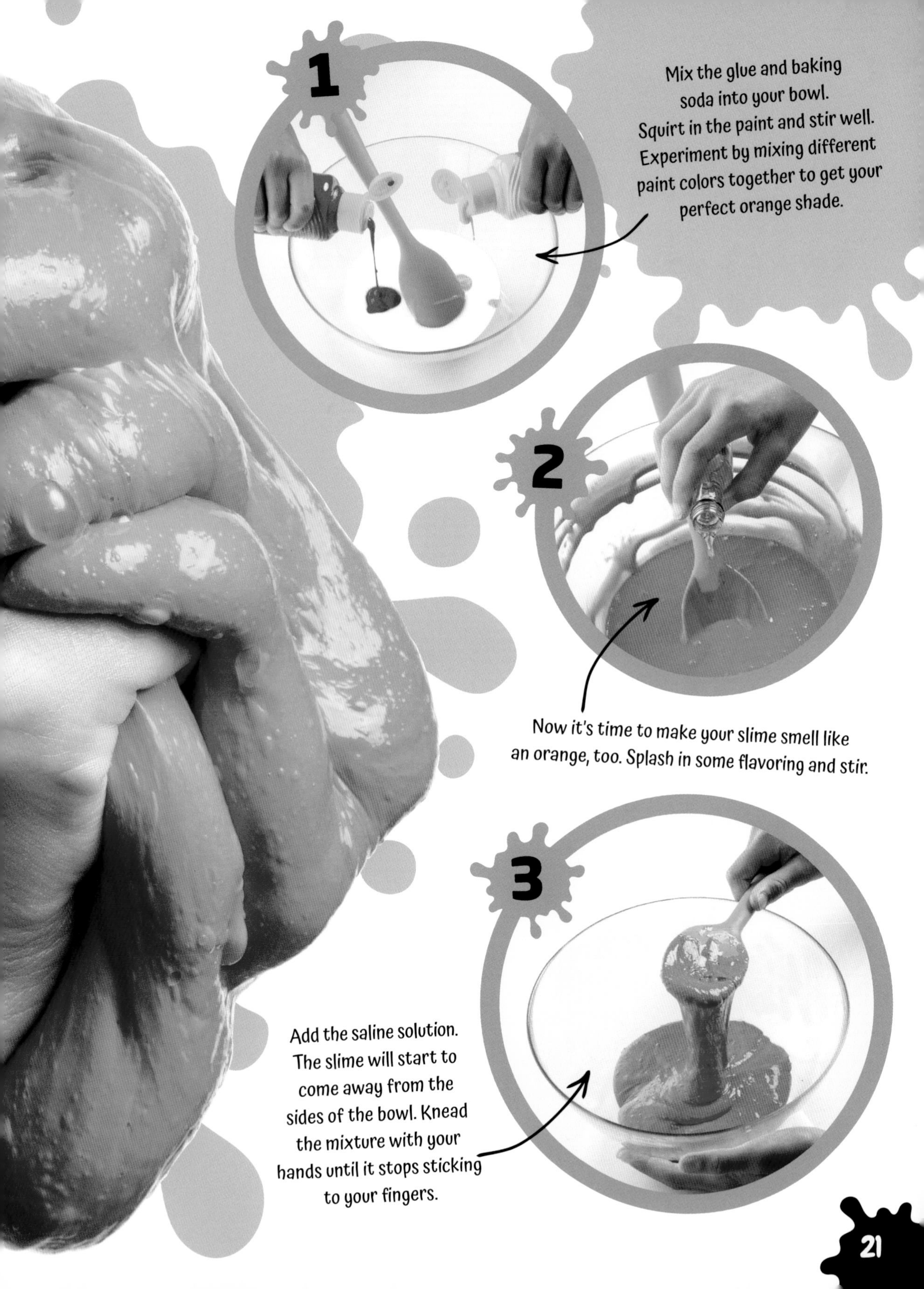

1

Mix the glue and baking soda into your bowl. Squirt in the paint and stir well. Experiment by mixing different paint colors together to get your perfect orange shade.

2

Now it's time to make your slime smell like an orange, too. Splash in some flavoring and stir.

3

Add the saline solution. The slime will start to come away from the sides of the bowl. Knead the mixture with your hands until it stops sticking to your fingers.

Glitter Slime

You can add glitter to lots of slime recipes, but it sparkles best when added to see-through slime.

YOU WILL NEED

- 3 tbsp (or 3 packets of) peel-off face masks—they must contain polyvinyl alcohol
- glitter
- 1 tsp baking soda
- saline solution—it must contain boric acid or sodium borate

After emptying the face masks into a bowl, sprinkle in some glitter. Try adding different colors and sizes of glitter for extra sparkle.

Stir in the baking soda.

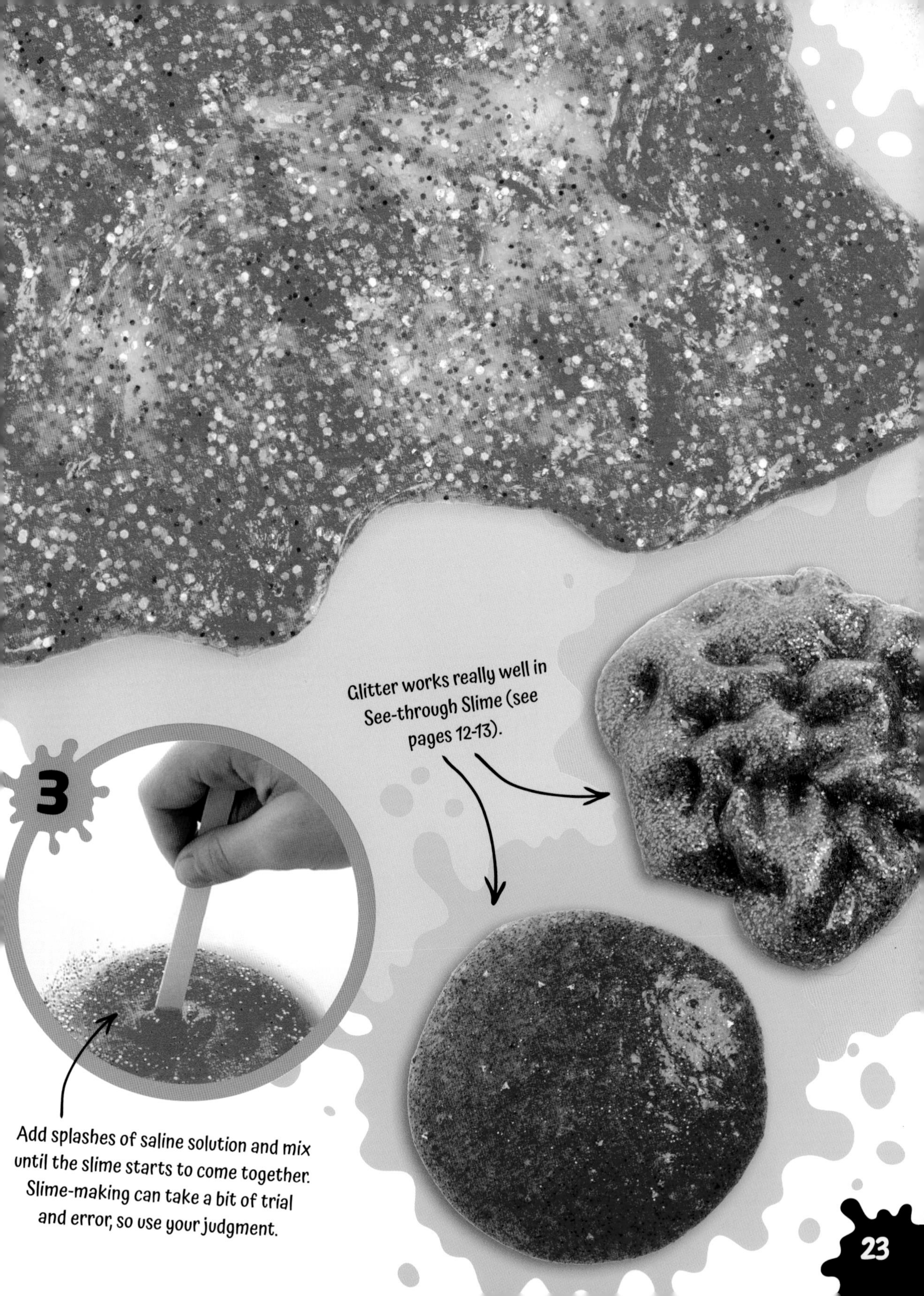
3
Glitter works really well in See-through Slime (see pages 12-13).
Add splashes of saline solution and mix until the slime starts to come together. Slime-making can take a bit of trial and error, so use your judgment.

Popping Slime

Want to make your slime go POP? This noisy slime looks like something spooky left behind by a ghost—oooohhhh!

YOU WILL NEED

- a couple of drops of green food coloring
- ½ tsp baking soda
- ½ cup warm water
- ⅔ cup clear craft glue
- saline solution—it must contain boric acid or sodium borate
- popping candy

1

Put two or three drops of green food coloring into a mixture of baking soda, water, and glue.

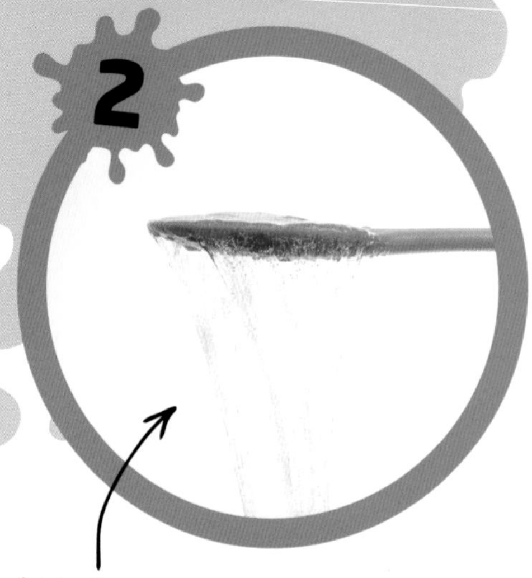

2

Add saline solution little by little until your slime gets stringy and starts to come away from the sides of the bowl.

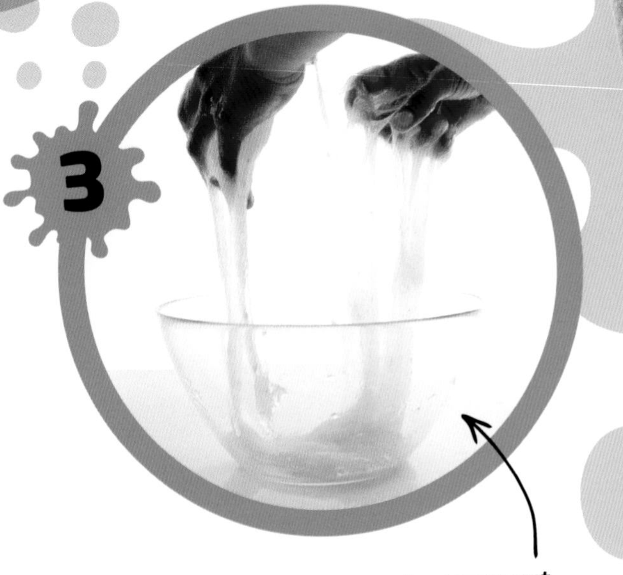

3

Sprinkle in as much popping candy as you want, then stick your hands in the bowl and mix everything together. Your slime will start popping as you play with it.

1
Leave your first batch paint-free!
Add ½ tsp of paint to your second batch.
Add 1 tsp of paint to your third batch.
Lastly, add 2 tbsp of paint to your fourth batch!
Put ½ cup glue and ½ tsp baking soda into each of your four bowls. Add different amounts of the same color paint to three of the batches.
2
After you have stirred in the paint, add in ½ tbsp of saline solution to each bowl to make the slime form.
3
Layer up your colors or shades and twist them around.
TOP TIP!
Any slime with stripes won't stay stripy for long. The more you play with your slime, the more the colors will blend together.

TIME:
10 MINUTES

DIFFICULTY:
EASY

WARNING:
NONEDIBLE

Gold Slime

If you're not careful, your gold slime might end up a nasty brown mess! Add some sparkly jewels to give your slime extra bling.

YOU WILL NEED

- ½ tsp baking soda
- ½ cup warm water
- ⅔ cup clear craft glue
- gold poster paint
- saline solution—it must contain boric acid or sodium borate
- plastic jewels or beads

1

Mix together the baking soda, water, and glue. Squirt in gold paint and stir until you're happy with the shade.

2

Add the saline solution little by little and stir until the slime comes together.

3

Sprinkle the plastic jewels or beads on the top of the mixture and fold them in using your hands. Now play!

If you can't find gold paint, why not try some gold glitter to really make your slime shine?

TOP TIP!

Use clear glue to get the best result when mixing with gold paint. Don't forget to wash your hands when finished!

Unicorn Slime

This super-fluffy unicorn slime is the biggest challenge yet. It makes more slime than any other recipe in this book!

YOU WILL NEED

FOR EACH SLIME COLOR:

- 2 cups shaving cream (not gel)
- food coloring (try yellow, blue, green, and red)
- 1/4 cup PVA glue
- 1/4 tsp baking soda
- 1 tbsp saline solution—it must contain boric acid or sodium borate
- glitter

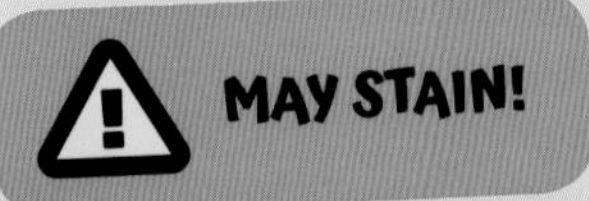

1 Make four batches of Fluffy Slime (see pages 10-11 for the method). Use a different food coloring for each mixture.

2

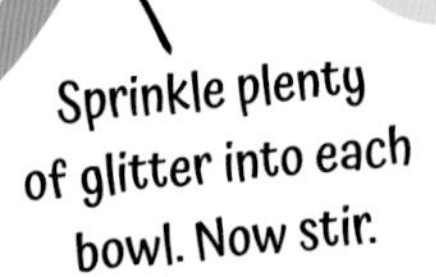

Sprinkle plenty of glitter into each bowl. Now stir.

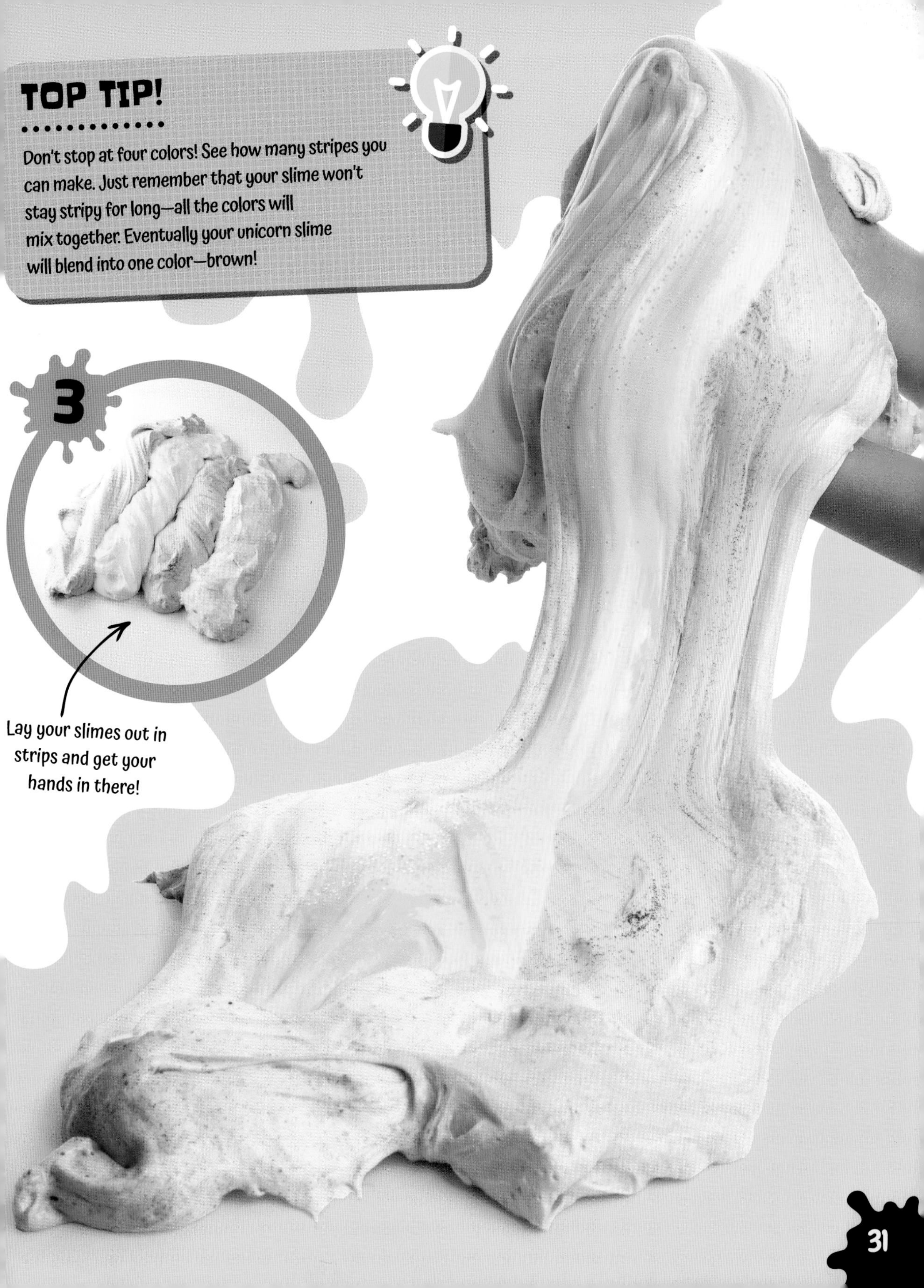

TOP TIP!

Don't stop at four colors! See how many stripes you can make. Just remember that your slime won't stay stripy for long—all the colors will mix together. Eventually your unicorn slime will blend into one color—brown!

3

Lay your slimes out in strips and get your hands in there!

Metallic Slime

TIME:
10 MINUTES

DIFFICULTY:
EASY

WARNING:
NONEDIBLE

Seek out special ingredients like luster dust to give your slime a real shine!

YOU WILL NEED

- ½ tsp baking soda
- ½ cup warm water
- ⅔ cup clear craft glue
- luster dust
- saline solution—it must contain boric acid or sodium borate

1

Mix together the baking soda, water, and clear glue. Sprinkle plenty of luster dust on top.

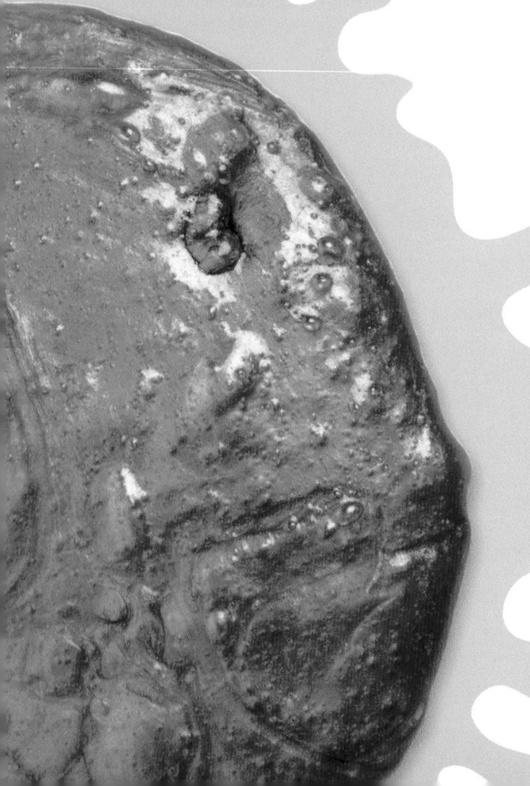

2

You won't need any additional color for this slime—the dust should be all you need. Stir it in.

3

Add drops of saline solution a little at a time. As you stir, your mixture will start to gloop together. When it comes away from the sides of the bowl, your slime is ready for some serious stretching!

TOP TIP!

There are lots of interesting ingredients that can take your slime making to the next level. Keep your eyes peeled for cake decorating items like luster dust (but don't be tempted to eat these). It's the little extras that will give your slime the personal touch!

MAY STAIN!

Sand Slime

TIME:
10 MINUTES

DIFFICULTY:
EASY

WARNING:
NONEDIBLE

There are loads of ways to add texture to your slime. Here is one of the simplest.

YOU WILL NEED

- ½ tsp baking soda
- ½ cup warm water
- ⅔ cup clear craft glue
- yellow food coloring
- saline solution—it must contain boric acid or sodium borate
- play sand

SCIENCE BIT

Sand is made when rocks are broken down into small grains. It comes in lots of different colors and textures. Did you know that the color of sand varies because of the kind of rock that it comes from?

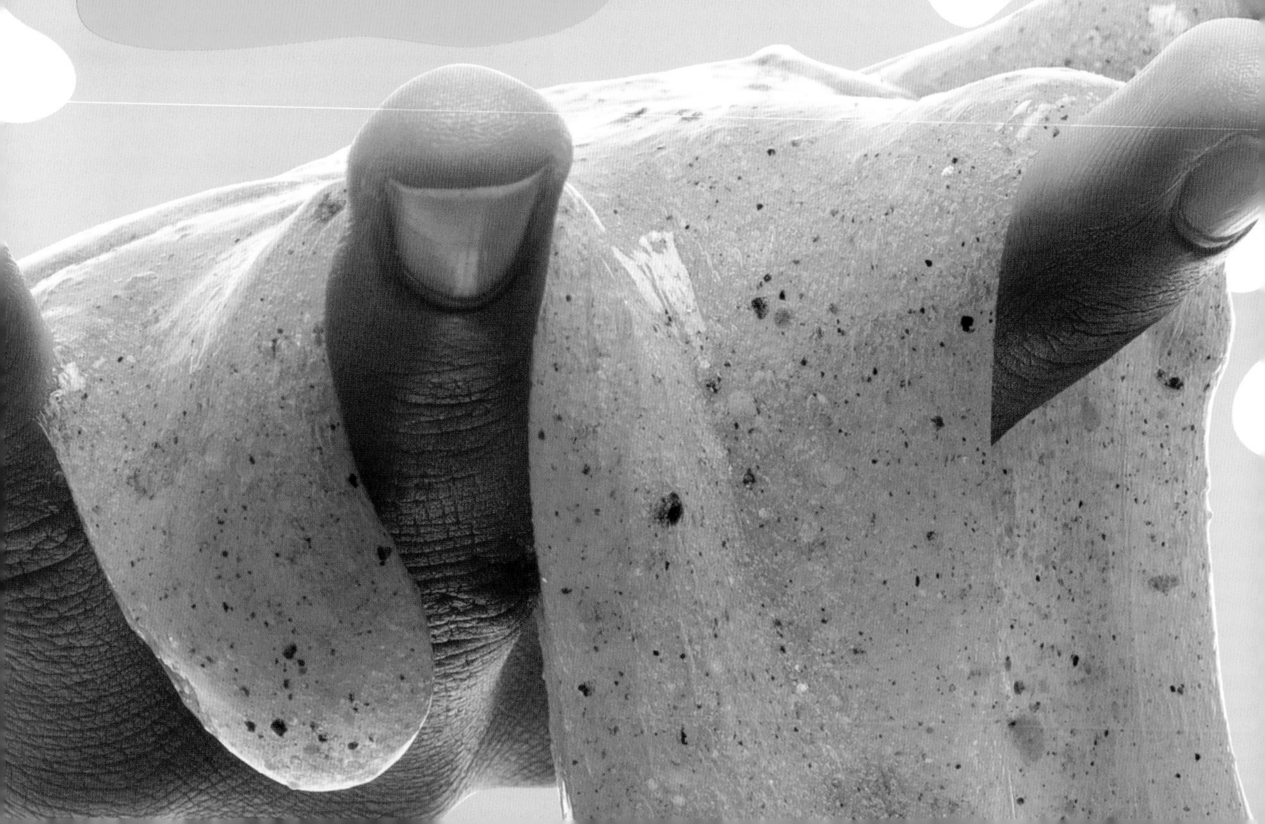

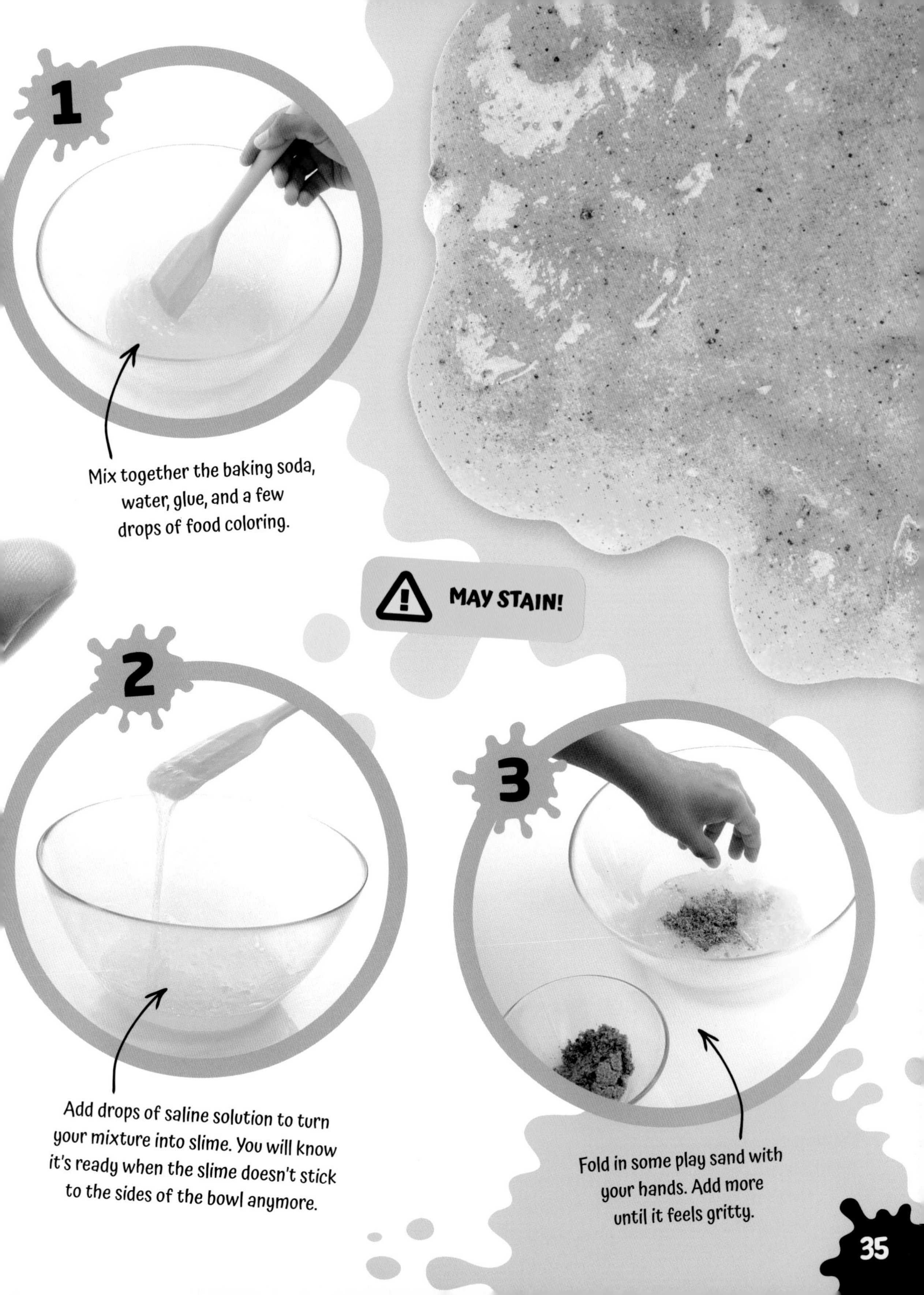
1
Mix together the baking soda, water, glue, and a few drops of food coloring.
MAY STAIN!
2
Add drops of saline solution to turn your mixture into slime. You will know it's ready when the slime doesn't stick to the sides of the bowl anymore.
3
Fold in some play sand with your hands. Add more until it feels gritty.

Monster Slime

Add googly eyes for awesome slime that looks like a melted monster!

YOU WILL NEED

- about ½ cup PVA glue
- ½ tsp baking soda
- green finger paint, or a mix of blue and yellow finger paints
- ½ tbsp saline solution—it must contain boric acid or sodium borate
- googly eyes

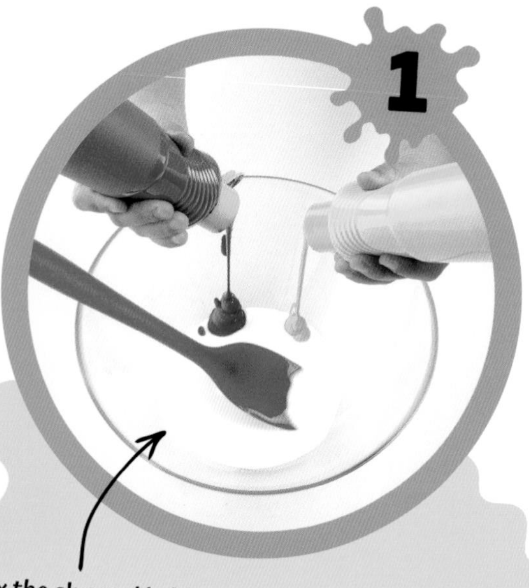

1

Mix the glue and baking soda. Squirt in blue and yellow paint. Keep mixing. Getting the right shade of green will be a bit of an experiment in color. Or if you have it, just use green paint!

2

Beat in the saline solution. You'll know when the slime is coming together when it turns stringy.

TOP TIP!

Try other paint colors, or mix two colors together, for a swirly, melted mess of a monster!

When the slime doesn't stick to the bowl anymore, it's ready. Make a splat of slime on a plastic mat and add googly eyes to create your melted monster!

Snow Slime

YOU WILL NEED

- 1½-2 cups shaving cream (not gel)
- ¼ cup PVA glue
- ¼ tsp baking soda
- 1 tbsp saline solution—it must contain boric acid or sodium borate
- small styrofoam balls

TIME:
15 MINUTES

DIFFICULTY:
EASY

WARNING:
NONEDIBLE

1
Make half a batch of Fluffy Slime (see pages 10-11), but without food coloring.
2
Gradually fold in the styrofoam balls. The slime should hold them in place nicely. You can add as many balls as you like.
MAY STAIN!
Add paint to this recipe to get a great textured and colorful slime you'll love to squish!

TOP TIP!

Don't play with slime in a room with carpets! Stick to playing on hard floors, or even better, go outside. If you drop any blobs, white vinegar should dissolve any dried-in slime accidents.

Fake Snot

TIME:
2 HOURS

DIFFICULTY:
INTERMEDIATE

WARNING:
NONEDIBLE

Time for a super-slimy, revolting recipe. It's perfect for Halloween or to gross out your family and friends! Just make sure a grown-up helps you with the boiling water.

YOU WILL NEED

- 1/2 cup boiling water
- 3 tsp gelatin
- green food coloring
- 1/4 cup corn syrup

SCIENCE BIT

Snot may not look pretty, but it's super useful. It stops germs and dust from being sucked up our noses and down into our lungs.

1 Ask a grown-up to carefully pour hot water into the small bowl and sprinkle the gelatin on top. Stir together with a fork.

BOILING WATER!

2

Next, add the food coloring. Drop in a splash at a time until you get a snotty shade of green. Don't touch the mixture until it has cooled for about an hour.

The green mixture will start to form a jelly. Slowly add it to a bowl with the corn syrup in. The slime should create strings of snotlike substance. Yuk!

Pompom Slime

TIME:
10 MINUTES

DIFFICULTY:
EASY

WARNING:
NONEDIBLE

See-through slime looks even better when you accessorize it! Try out this cool way of adding color and texture.

YOU WILL NEED

- ½ tsp baking soda
- ½ cup warm water
- ⅔ cup clear craft glue
- saline solution—it must contain boric acid or sodium borate
- packet of mini pompoms

1

Make up a batch of See-through Slime (see pages 12-13). You don't need to wait a week to use this mixture though. The bubbles add to the look!

2
Empty a packet of pompoms into the slime. Fold them in using your hands.
3
See how far your polka-dot slime can stretch!
MAY STAIN!

How about...?

Add plastic alphabet tiles to your slime rather than pompoms. Then squish the slime about to make words or your name. Don't add too many pieces though—they'll fall out!

Winter Wonderland Slime

This is a simple and quick way to theme your slime. Vary it with different wintry colors and confetti. Unleash your imagination!

YOU WILL NEED

- ½ tsp baking soda
- ½ cup warm water
- ⅔ cup mixture of clear craft glue and light-blue glitter glue
- saline solution—it must contain boric acid or sodium borate
- snowflake confetti
- extra glitter (optional)

Try this one after mastering See-thr
Slime (see pages 12-13). This version u
part clear glue and part glitter glue,
the recipe is just the same, and you do
need to wait for the bubbles to clear

Fold in the snowflake confetti. The super thing about slime is there is no right or wrong when it comes to adding extras. You can put in as much or as little confetti as you like.

If you don't think your slime has enough sparkle, fold in a big sprinkle of glitter.

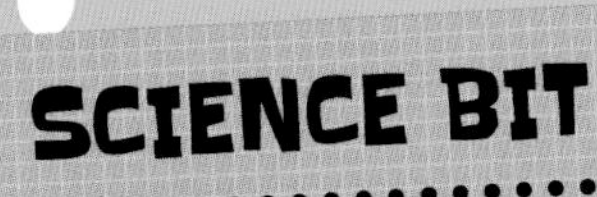

This type of snowflake is also known as a snow crystal. No two snow crystals look the same. This is because their patterns depend on how they fall through clouds.

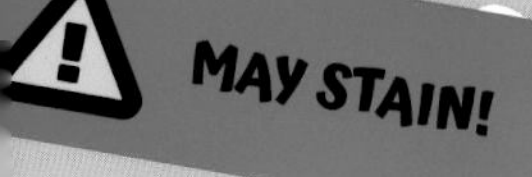

Dinosaurs in Amber

Discover dinosaur treasures hidden deep inside this prehistoric slime!

YOU WILL NEED

- ½ tsp baking soda
- ½ cup warm water
- ⅔ cup clear craft glue
- yellow food coloring
- yellow glitter
- gold luster dust
- saline solution—it must contain boric acid or sodium borate
- small plastic dinosaur toys

1

Add food coloring, glitter, and luster dust to a mixture of baking soda, water, and glue. Make sure you don't add too much food coloring— the color shouldn't be overpowering.

2

Beat in the saline solution until the amber mixture becomes stringy and comes away from the bowl.

3

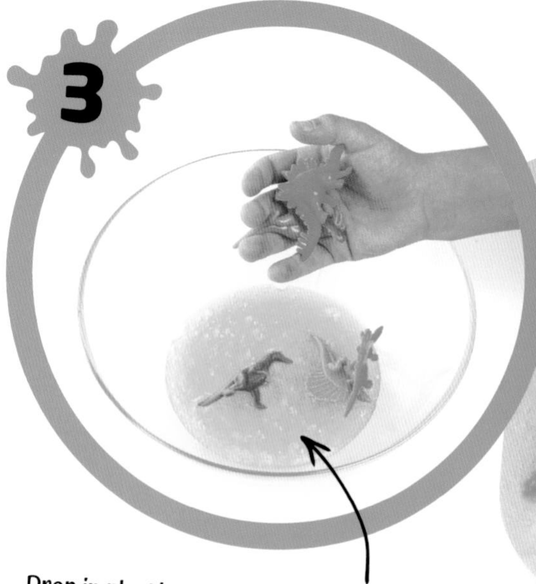

Drop in plastic dinosaur toys and see if your slime is sticky enough for them not to fall out.

TIME:
10 MINUTES

DIFFICULTY:
EASY

WARNING:
NONEDIBLE

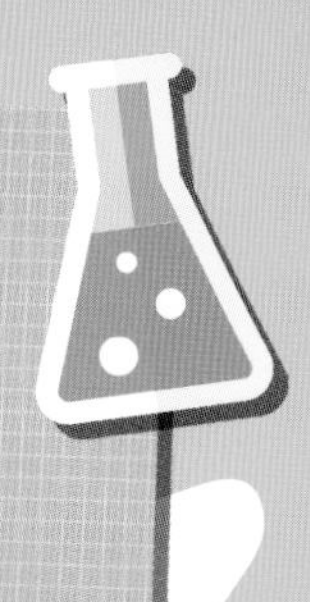

SCIENCE BIT

Amber is a liquid that oozes from prehistoric trees and then becomes as hard as rock over time. Ancient insect and dinosaur parts have been found trapped inside lumps of amber!

MAY STAIN!

Bubbling Swamp Slime

TIME:
2–3 HOURS

DIFFICULTY:
INTERMEDIATE

WARNING:
NONEDIBLE

Mixing baking soda and vinegar makes this slime bubble—this is called a chemical reaction. The result is a slime that belongs on an alien planet!

YOU WILL NEED

- 2 cups white vinegar
- 1¼ tsp xanthan gum
- green food coloring or a mix of other colors to make a murky green color
- baking soda

1

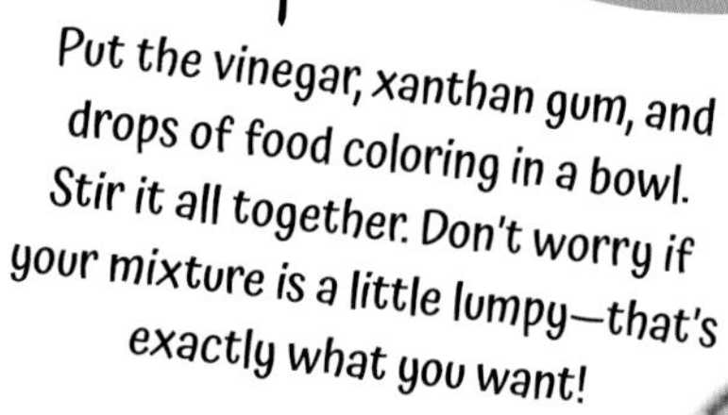

Put the vinegar, xanthan gum, and drops of food coloring in a bowl. Stir it all together. Don't worry if your mixture is a little lumpy—that's exactly what you want!

SCIENCE BIT

This slime is bubbly because of the way vinegar and baking soda react to each other. They produce carbon dioxide. You could also use lemon juice instead of vinegar since it is an acid, too!

Once you've finished stirring your mixture, put it in the fridge for a few hours until it has thickened.

Place a thick layer of baking soda in the bottom of a clean bowl, then cover it with the green gloop. Bubbles will pop up through the mix and glug away for some time.

MAY STAIN!

Bubble Slime

Slime is not just for stretching and squishing... why not try blowing bubbles with it?

YOU WILL NEED

- about 1 cup PVA glue
- 1 tsp baking soda
- pink food coloring
- 1 tbsp saline solution—it must contain boric acid or sodium borate

1. Make up a batch of Stretchy Slime (see pages 8-9), but this time use pink food coloring.

2. Stick a straw in the slime. Pinch around the edges at the bottom to make sure the straw is air-tight. This means no air can escape through the hole.

3. Blow slowly and steadily to make the biggest bubble you can! When it pops, reposition your straw and blow another one.

Edible Slime

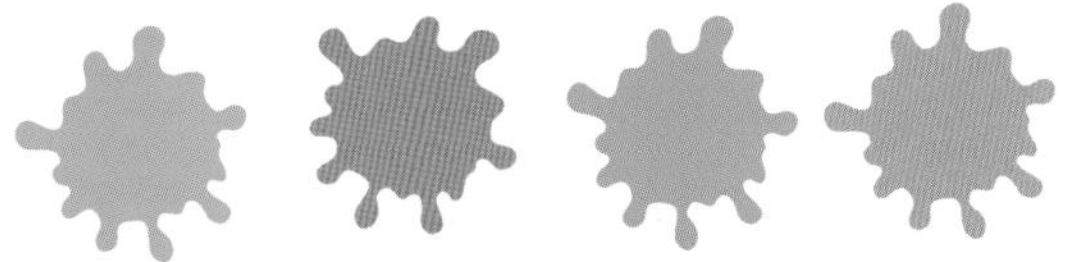

Make sure you have plenty of cornstarch to keep these slimes from sticking to surfaces, and to you! Grab an adult when making these recipes—hot equipment is needed. Always check with a grown-up before handling slimes that have been heated and eat within 24 hours.

Chocolate Goo

Perfect for playing a trick on someone, this slime looks yucky, but tastes yummy!

YOU WILL NEED

- ½ x 14-ounce can condensed milk
- 2 tbsp chocolate sauce
- 1 tbsp cornstarch

1

Empty half a can of condensed milk into a saucepan. Add the chocolate sauce and stir in well.

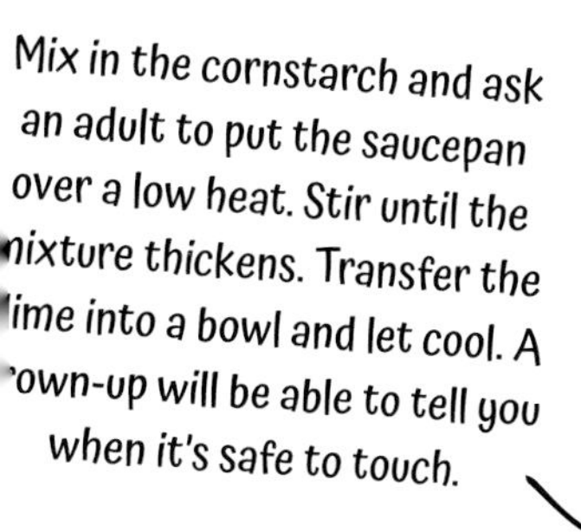

Mix in the cornstarch and ask an adult to put the saucepan over a low heat. Stir until the nixture thickens. Transfer the lime into a bowl and let cool. A own-up will be able to tell you when it's safe to touch.

3

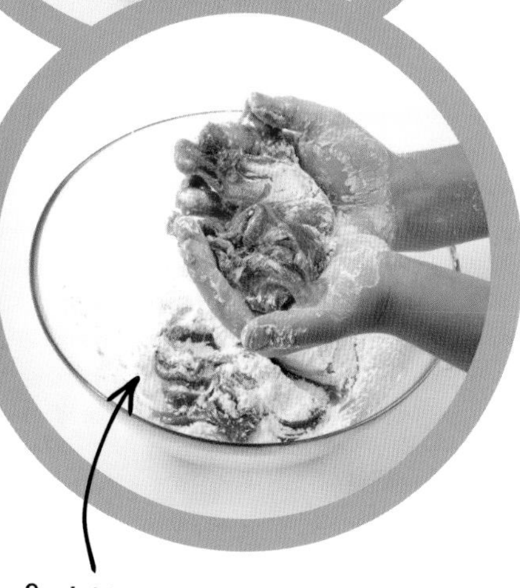

Sprinkle cornstarch over your slime, then onto your hands, too. This will help it not stick to you quite so much. Then get in there and squish that slime!

How about..?

Try adding some tasty, crunchy snacks to the slime. Chocolate chips will go down a treat and make it even more chocolatey! Or maybe raisins or dried fruit? Add a handful in Step 3 when the slime has cooled down enough to be squished.

Sticky, Icky, Tasty Slime

TIME:
10 MINUTES

DIFFICULTY:
INTERMEDIATE

WARNING:
EDIBLE SLIME

Some of the recipes in this book look good enough to eat, but you definitely shouldn't eat them. However, this one is completely edible. Yum!

YOU WILL NEED

- **package of marshmallows—we used 10 big marshmallows, but you can try this with as many or as few as you like**
- **a couple of spoonfuls of cornstarch**
- **a couple of spoonfuls of confectioners' sugar**

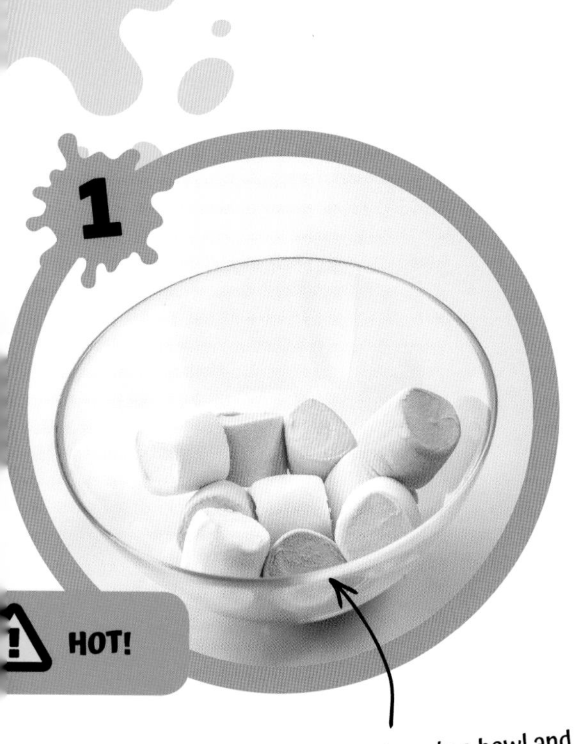

1

HOT!

Place your marshmallows in a bowl and ask an adult to microwave on full power for 10 seconds. Repeat until melted. Don't touch yet as it'll be mega hot! Wait a few minutes for the mixture to cool.

2

HOT!

Sprinkle over equal amounts of cornstarch and confectioners' sugar. Add them a little at a time—not too much or your slime will be too tough to handle and might not taste as good. Stir together using a spoon. No touching! It's still hot.

3

Get a grown-up to test the temperature of the slime. If it's nice and cool, stick your hands in and enjoy. Don't eat it all at once!

TOP TIP!

This is much stickier than most slime recipes. The best thing is that you can lick your hands clean when you've finished playing with this one! Just remember to wash your hands before making and handling this slime. And always clean up after yourself!

The Bear Necessities

Melting sweets makes a slime that smells and tastes delicious. Melted gummy bears end up more like a putty than a slime!

YOU WILL NEED

* a few packages of gummy bears
* cornstarch
* confectioners' sugar

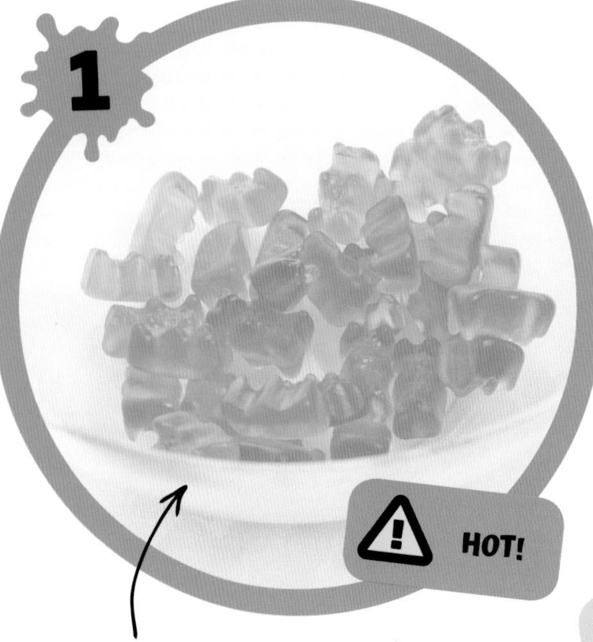

Pick out all of the bears of your favorite color. Put them in a bowl and ask an adult to microwave on full power for 10 seconds. Repeat until they've all melted.

You will have a lovely, glassy, melted mixture, but watch out—it will be super-hot! Stir it carefu with a spoon, or ask a grown up to help.

TOP TIP!

The amount of cornstarch and confectioners' sugar needed depends on how many gummy bears you use. Start off with little spoonfuls and increase until you've got it just right. The cornstarch keeps the slime from sticking to you, but the confectioners' sugar keeps it tasting sweet!

2

Sprinkle a mixture of confectioners' sugar and cornstarch onto a clean surface. Spoon out each bowl of melted candies onto the dusted surface to cool. Ask a grown-up to let you know when the blobs are cool enough to handle.

3

Sprinkle more confectioners' sugar and cornstarch on top of each blob. Roll each color into a long sausage shape. Layer the colors and twist them around. When you've had enough, just take a bite!

TOP TIP!

Make sure you have plenty of cornstarch to keep this slime from sticking to surfaces, and to you! The more you stretch it, the less sticky it should become.

Slime Storage

You need to look after your slime carefully to keep it from drying out. Make sure you store your slime in an airtight container and in the refrigerator once you've finished playing to keep it clean and slimy. Your slime may turn your container a different shade, so only use a tub that you're allowed to!

plastic boxes with lids

Cleaning Up

You won't be popular if you make a mess, so follow these rules...

- Always make slime on a wipe-clean surface.
- There's always a risk of staining with paint or food coloring, so lay down some paper first.
- Mop up and clean up as soon as you can.
- Wash hands before and after handling slime.
- Wipe down all surfaces and put your slime kit and ingredients away.
- NEVER pour slime failures down the sink—you'll block the drains!
- Always ask an adult before using cleaning products to wipe up.

Hints and Tips

The recipes in this book should be easy to make, but slightly different ingredients may change the texture of the slime. With a bit of trial and error you should be able to get the results you want, but here are a few pointers.

MY GLUE-BASED SLIME IS TOO STICKY!
Add a few more drops of saline and mix in well. Keep adding until the right consistency.

MY EDIBLE SLIME IS TOO STICKY!
Cover your hands with cornstarch or add more into the mix, but remember the mess is part of the fun!

MY SLIME BREAKS WHEN I STRETCH IT!
Sounds like you've added too much saline. Try squirting a small amount of the glue you've used onto your slime and carefully fold it in.

MY SLIME ISN'T GLITTERY ENOUGH!
If you're using PVA glue, make sure you've got a chunky glitter rather than a fine one otherwise it will get lost. And remember the key rule when making a glittery slime—add some glitter, then add some more!

MY SLIME IS GETTING HARD!
Slime doesn't last forever! If kept in an airtight container and in the refrigerator, it may last for up to a week, then it will need to be thrown away. Edible slime will be yummy for a day. Then it's time to make the next slime!